Have Lipstick, Will Travel
How to reimagine your life, purpose & hair color!

Also by Annette Bridges

The Gospel According to Mamma:
One mother's philosophy on love, money, God, aging,
decisions, change, and much more

Be Queen of Your Life
A savvy mom helps daughters command and rule their lives

Lady and Bella:
Totally different, Totally friends

Lady and Bella's Alphabet Kitchen:
A to Z Recipes for Kid Cooks

Have Lipstick, Will Travel

How to reimagine your life, purpose & hair color!

Annette Bridges

Have Lipstick, Will Travel
© 2015 by Ranch House Press. All rights reserved.
Printed in the United States of America.

www.annettebridges.com

ISBN-13: 978-0-9976014-2-8

*Dedicated to women wondering
what in the hell
to do next in their lives.*

"To travel is to take a journey into yourself."
—Danny Kaye

Contents

xi | Preface
xv | Introduction
1 | Part One: Coral Bliss
17 | Part Two: Bronze Treasure
35 | Part Three: Frozen Rose
53 | Part Four: Rich Ruby
81 | Part Five: Fuchsia Fever

102 | Lipstick Ladies League
105 | Acknowledgments

Illustrations
"Lipstick Pearls"

xxi | Never underestimate
15 | Today is big
33 | When you can't change
51 | Opportunities begin
78 | It's never too late

Preface

My quest to reimagine my life, purpose, and hair color began with many earth-shattering questions that stirred in my heart when I became an empty nester. But for the record, although an empty-nest mom writes this book, that doesn't mean that its messages are only of interest to other empty nesters. On the contrary, the ideas in this book are for women of all ages trying to understand their life purpose, discover their passion, and find their voice. I don't believe you need to wait until midlife to embark on a voyage to your ultimate, dream-inspired, goal-motivated transformation. That said, it's never too late to begin a life-changing rock-your-world journey!

Before my questions came my quandary. I knew my world was about to change. I had been anticipating and dreading the moment for over a year. My only child was college-bound, for fall 2001. I could not imagine my world without my daughter's daily presence. We had homeschooled for the past eight years so there was rarely an hour we weren't together. Even when she went to summer camp, I went with her and volunteered.

The day arrived all too soon for her to begin her life away at college. It was inevitable, and I had to face it. The time had finally arrived for me to let her go—without going with her.

I felt alone, lost, and isolated. Living on a 400-acre cattle ranch in Texas fueled my feelings of loneliness. My shopping companion, movie buddy, confidant, and best friend was no longer with me. *Thank God for cell phones,* I thought to myself, remembering what it was like when I went to college in the 1970s and at most had a weekly conversation with my mom on a phone shared with fifty other women.

But even though it was possible to communicate with my daughter daily, I didn't want to be being in touch obsessively. I wanted her to focus on her own life, purpose, and goals. It was time for me to reimagine mine.

What would that look like? What could that look like? What was I going to do with my time each day? What did I want to do? What was I qualified to do?

Two weeks after my daughter left when I was only beginning to ask myself these questions and get a little more sleep, I woke up on September 11th to the attack on our country. In my horror watching that second plane fly into the World Trade Center, I wished my daughter were home. When I finally reached her on the telephone, her alarm was already as high as mine because her roommate's dad was at the Pentagon when the plane attacked there. Her roommate was overwhelmed with fear trying to reach him (she eventually made contact with him and learned he was safe).

The days and nights that followed brought even more fears and feelings of inadequacy at being able to keep my child safe. The helplessness and uncertainty were powerful. As months passed and the stories of loved ones lost in that horrific attack filled our airwaves, I thought more and more about the life lessons that I had tried to share and instill in my daughter. Had I done enough? Had I taught her everything she needed to be prepared for the crazy, violent world she was now facing?

These questions, along with listening to the concerns others in our country were raising, led to my first newspaper column published in the *Dallas Morning News* at Christmastime after 9/11. I wanted to share a vivid childhood Christmas memory that included living through a violent and unstable time while still finding happiness in the achievement of new goals.

I would write hundreds of newspaper and magazine columns during the first ten years of my daughter's life away from home. Life's seasons and events inspired topics. I hoped that what I shared was helpful to whoever read them, but I really hoped I was leaving a written legacy for my daughter. I knew she would not always have her mom around. That may sound a bit morbid, but in the beginning of my writing years that was a primary motivation.

I went from a brand new empty-nest mom wondering what in the hell I was going to do next to being a prolific writer. There was no big plan, no business goals. I simply wrote.

That first decade was followed by a few turbulent years involving deaths of loved ones from cancer and from alcoholism as well as my own health problems resulting in two surgeries. My newspaper writing came to a sudden halt. But it was during these sad and scary years that my book publishing began.

While recovering from my first surgery, I had lots of sofa time on my hands. Coming face to face with fears of death has a way of making a gal rather reflective on her life. I decided to reread every column I had written and notice the evolution of insights gleaned. You might say it was a connecting of dots in my life. The epigraph in my first book was this quote by Ralph Waldo Emerson: "Life is a succession of lessons which must be lived to be understood." I agree! With the re-reading of my life lessons in print, a surprising clarity emerged.

Grateful to have my aging mother still with me, I was compelled to write a book about her. I wanted to thank her for being my mamma and make her feel appreciated and important to me. As I read over my writings, I saw how often I either quoted my sweet mamma or shared wisdom she taught me. She has always been a huge role model for me of strength, courage and persistence. I had to share her story and lessons learned with others. I didn't know anything about book publishing, but I became passionately compelled to journey into this unknown territory. My daughter inspired my next book in what I hoped would be a pertinent guidepost especially for young women as they endeavored to reach for their dreams.

And so it was during my years of illness and loss that the inspiration for this book emerged. I had an urgent feeling that I needed to reimagine my life and purpose—that I needed to discover new passion and find my voice. I wasn't happy with myself. I had gained weight. I wasn't physically active, spending most of my waking hours sitting at my desk. I didn't like the woman I saw looking back at me in the mirror. My mind was filled with more questions and everywhere I went I hoped to discover answers. Somehow I felt the answers I was looking for were waiting for me somewhere out there in our great big world. And so, the search began . . .

Introduction

Why lipstick? Maybe because I've always insisted that "change your lipstick, change your life" is much more than a metaphor.

Every woman probably has that little something she carries around with her that brings her security or boosts her confidence. Maybe you have a favorite pair of shoes that make you feel extra glamorous. Or a scarf that makes you feel bold and daring. Or a special ring from a special someone you know loves you. You get the idea.

For me, it's almost always been about lipstick. Finding that perfect shade helps me feel whatever it is I'm needing to feel in that moment. Brave! Sexy! Youthful! Adventurous! Whatever!

Yes, it's amazing what a splash of color on your lips can do for you. A switch in the shade you've worn for years can completely alter your outlook. Whether you need a new job or a new man, painting your lips with fresh color can empower you to apply for the job you thought you could never get or give you the courage to make a difficult decision.

When I was five years old, I was blessed with a mamma who was also the local Avon lady. What this meant to my kindergartener self was access to hundreds of lipsticks. My mamma kept her trays of samples in her dresser drawer, and this was no secret to me. I have many fond memories of standing on my stool in front of Mamma's dresser so I could look in the mirror as I tried out the plethora of colors. At a surprisingly young age, it became my daily ritual to figure out which hue was perfect for my day or occasion. I grew up believing that painting my lips was as necessary as brushing my teeth.

There is nothing I do in my life today at fifty-something that doesn't require a dollop of lipstick first—whether I'm heading to the gym to work out or driving a tractor in a hayfield on our cattle ranch. Or even if I'm cozying on the sofa with my sweet husband watching television, you can bet my lips have the appropriate glisten.

After our only child left home for college, I knew I needed a radical revision of my choices of lipstick—among other things. As I embarked on brand new daily routines, my antiquated lipsticks were not giving me the pristine perspective I now desperately needed.

Besides different lipstick colors, I needed different hobbies, adventures, and clothes, along with a new hairdo and a new body size. A revision of my attitude and eating habits would also be required as I wrote this next chapter in my life.

One thing was certain—I was hungry and ready to fill my plate with anything and everything contemporary, fashionable, novel, and virgin. Wherever I was, whether at home or traveling, I was an eager student demanding that life teach me something new. I needed answers to my questions.

What was my passion and purpose? Where could I find my voice and the meaning of my life? Not to belittle motherhood, but was being a mother my sole life purpose? Surely there was more for me to accomplish. I felt compelled to make some changes but didn't know where to begin. So with expectant eyes and exciting and glistening lips everywhere I traversed, I learned astounding and marvelous lessons that changed my life again and again.

You, my lady friends, can do the same! Get rid of your outdated lipstick shades and add pizzazz to your life with some kick-ass colors. Then hit the road with a revitalized you! But be prepared—there's a wonder-filled world out there waiting. Anything can happen when you're open and ready to learn, change, and grow.

Are you ready to begin your reimagined life? Start with a trip to your closest makeup counter and pick out a shade of lipstick you've never worn before. Or, you can email me and I'll mail you an Avon sample to try. Really!

Next, listen to the Disney song, "A Whole New World" from the Aladdin movie. Yes, you heard me right. I'm recommending a Disney song. (I came by my Disney passion right at birth, when my mamma named me after the Disney Mouseketeer Annette Funicelo.)

Listen carefully to the song's words. Imagine you are Princess Jasmine and Aladdin is singing to you when he asks the question, "When did you last let your heart decide?" Imagine that you are about to embark on a magic carpet ride into a whole new world, and you're going to get "a new fantastic point of view."

Then travel with me as I embark to familiar and sometimes unknown territories; experience my stories of lessons learned and insights gleaned; hear my tales of self-discovery; and read this narrative about a mother/daughter/sister/aunt/wife who finally understands her real self—and that coping with change and conquering fears are easier when wearing a brand new shade of lipstick.

My book is divided into five colorful parts: Coral Bliss, Bronze Treasure, Frozen Rose, Rich Ruby, and Fuchsia Fever. You'll learn what each lipstick color signifies to me and what it can mean for you, too. Within each color part will be travels, insights, and lipstick pearls that I hope will be helpful as you set out to reimagine your life, purpose, and hair color.

Coral Bliss
Be who you truly are

Wearing Coral Bliss lipstick, those organic reddish or pinkish shades of orange, beckons the freedom of our inner spirit that encourages us to be who we truly are. Once we discover that, we know we are enough. We don't need to wish we could be different or like someone else.

You can authentically connect with your own life to become more of yourself. It's not really about the need to change yourself, but rather becoming more of who you are. Trust that you are enough right now. Listen to your inner voice and not the opinions of others.

The calm and confidence from wearing the coral shades of lipstick will enable you to discover a self that has been hidden by the drudgery of life's obligations and responsibilities. No more diminishing of yourself or allowing others to diminish you. You have to know who you are to be who you are. So dab on some Coral Bliss—or Tropical Coral or Silky Peach—and embark on an invigorating and empowering journey of self-awakening.

A lifetime of beach travels

When I need some self-awakening, I head to the ocean. It's where I find the peace I rarely experience anywhere else. I don't need much while I'm gazing out at the broad, radiant horizon, breathing soothing, salty sea air, and listening to the waves blissfully pound the shoreline—while I burrow my feet into the velvety smooth sand, I might add. (Well, perhaps there was a time when a dozen hot Krispy Kreme doughnuts would have been extra super nice!)

Yes, ma'am, I can sit for hours by the seaside completely enraptured by the boundlessness of the immense view. There's something about it that makes my soul sigh in contentment and quiets my mind in peaceful reflection.

Sitting on the seashore, I shut my heavy, burdened eyes, not thinking about any troubles, fears, or concerns. With each deep breath I take, I feel warmly wrapped in a divine love. I hear the thunderous roar of powerful waves crashing, but at the same time I feel the rhythmic and steady pattern of the steady waves rolling in. I feel as if a voice is whispering, "You are safe. You are not alone. Everything is going to be okay." I open my surprised eyes once again to the expansive scene before me. Whatever problem had been troubling me now seems very small, like a single grain of sand under my feet. There is clarity, and there is calm.

Throughout my childhood, my mamma thought a trip to the ocean was a cure for anything. Of course, my Avon Lady mamma also believed a new shade of lipstick was a similar cure! Anytime we were struggling with some difficulty or had a major decision looming, Mamma would paint her lips with a new color and take us to the beach in search of peace or direction. Eventually, I associated peace of mind, body, and spirit as only truly possible when I was by the sea, preferably with coral tinted lips.

A new outlook on life

I was sitting in my sand chair, on the beach of my dreams in Pensacola, Florida, listening to the tranquil surf and taking slow, deep breaths of the soothing, salty sea air, reading my magazine—with glistening Coral Bliss lips of course—away from ringing phones and other distractions. Life was pretty good that Labor Day Weekend 2001. This was my first trip to the beach with my husband as empty-nest parents, and honestly, we were remembering how fun it was to spend time with just the two of us. Little did I suspect I was soon to read a captivating story that would lead me to question my entire outlook.

Why is it that a near-death experience often leads to a dramatic change of course?

The story was about a change in the life trajectory of a certain couple. They were in the eighth year of a five-year plan to accomplish their dream of a life at sea. After the wife had had a serious health scare, they had asked the question, "What are we waiting for?" They had answered by putting lucrative careers on hold and selling everything that wouldn't fit on a sailboat. Thus began their change of course.

The first thing that hit me was that I didn't have a five-year plan, or a ten-year plan, or any plan at all for the rest of my empty-nest life. I had reached middle age practically overnight, without making new goals or imagining new dreams. I had even lapsed into wearing the same shade of lipstick for longer than I could remember. Somewhere along the way, I had stopped envisioning or planning for the future and stopped shopping for new lipsticks. I had my trusty favorite and that seemed sufficient. So this beach trip was a long-overdue reunion for my lips and Coral Bliss!

After reading the couple's story, I asked myself what I wanted to do with the rest of my life. I was comfortable, content, and satisfied. But, a future of senior years was a path I wasn't anxious to travel, so I had focused only on making the most of present moments and was letting the future take care of itself.

My husband and I talked about places we wanted to see and things we wanted to do—"one of these days." But we didn't have specific dates in mind for these dreams. I now wondered if our dreams would ever be reached without setting tangible and realistic goals.

I recalled how the frustration and unhappiness from my younger days when I wanted to make a change but I didn't know where to go or how to begin. But I also remembered the wisdom gained from these times. I learned that a proactive and definitive approach was needed to make progress, rather than a vague proposal that kept me in idle, doing nothing, going nowhere.

Now, I wanted to change my view as well as my course for the future. As I sat in my trusty sand chair gazing upon the sweeping ocean scene before my eyes, I contemplated the infinitude of life. An elderly friend of a friend came to mind. This dear man was in the midst of remodeling his home, even though he was approaching the century mark. My friend asked him why he was remodeling. He replied, "I take my concept of home with me into eternity." He further explained how he must always be perfecting, improving, moving forward—setting goals and going about achieving the goals.

If you're a country music fan like me, perhaps you recall Tim McGraw's hit song, "Live Like You Were Dying." The song encourages listeners to live "like tomorrow was a gift" and to make the most of the present. This song got me to thinking.

My view of the rest of my life had become clouded by fear and dread. I had lost the zeal and joyful anticipation for the future I had felt in my youth when I gazed upon my mamma's drawer filled with millions of miniature lipsticks I thought had been made especially for me.

It was most certainly time to change my course and chart a fresh one, sing a new song, and put on new shades of lipstick frequently. To me this would mean expecting abundant prospects for what I might do next in my life. (McGraw's song suggests bull riding!)

I was being impelled to ponder my future with a new sense of enthusiasm and anticipation. I would reshape my view of the future into one without fear of age and tribulations, without limitations—one that encourages goal setting and an expectation of obtaining new dreams. It would be a future filled with exhilarating adventures and cutting-edge lipstick colors.

Underwater Awakening

I felt like I was visiting another world. I suppose that's exactly what my husband and I did when we toured the mysterious world under the deep, blue sea. During our trip to Maui in 2002, a day didn't go by without us snorkeling in the crystal-blue waters. It was a good thing I was prepared with waterproof Tropical Coral lipstick!

I couldn't help but think of and appreciate Jacques-Yves Cousteau. The goggles he designed enabled him to explore the breathtaking and awe-inspiring world under the sea. Now his invention was enabling us to do the same.

We were never alone in our fascination and exploration. Whether by boat or beach, we and our fellow adventurers respectfully entered the ocean to observe its domain. We were all immensely curious and reverent as we peered into a realm so unlike our own. There was a great desire to learn and understand more about this foreign underwater land and its inhabitants.

As I came eye to eye with many a fish, I wondered what they thought about their nosy intruders. I wanted to assure them to have no fear, that I would do them no harm—that I only wanted to observe and appreciate the beauty and uniqueness of their world. But they didn't seem to mind their onlookers as they continued about their business.

Wintertime in Maui meant seeing mother and baby humpback whales. We loved seeing and admiring these enormous and intriguing mammals. When scooting around the Maui waters and coming upon these beautiful creatures, boats immediately cut their engines so as not to harm them. Mamma and baby whales always got the right-of-way!

Our Maui expeditions made me ponder how truly wide the world is—filled with many different people and cultures, ambitions and tastes. I wondered if I could approach the rest of this great big world of ours with the same consideration, courtesy, and civility that we had given to our ocean friends.

We made every attempt not to disturb or harm the coral or any part of the ocean world when we visited. But did I give the same care or concern to the land upon which I lived?

When it came to people who had different interests from mine, different backgrounds, different opinions—or who were different from me in any way—did I have an earnest desire to know more about them? Did I sincerely want to understand why they thought the way they did? Did I give the same respect to other cultures that I had given to the underwater world, which was equally foreign to me?

I needed to let consideration, courtesy, and civility guide my attitudes and actions on land and sea in everything I did and with everyone I met. These life values should come as naturally to me on land as they do when I am snorkeling in the ocean. But I knew it would take more than another layer of coral color on my lips to make the transformation that was becoming part of my new life goals.

I made myself promises in Maui that would lead to better relationships and a happier me. Now, even in conversations with brothers, my husband, or my father-in-law, when they're expressing opposing points of view from mine, I became able to listen. I genuinely tried to understand their ideas and respect their feelings. It was no longer about me trying to change their minds or thinking they had to think the same as me. What a relief! It wasn't about who was wrong. After all, we both might have been! I finally learned that listening with respect, tolerance, and acceptance of multiple points of view creates joy, peace of mind, and happier relationships.

A bikini made just for you

It was spring break vacation in March 2005 with my daughter on the Alabama coast when I learned bikinis come in all shapes and sizes. That's right, ladies. Whatever your weight, height, or age, there's a bikini made for you.

As I sat in my sand chair (wearing my one piece), woman after woman in their bikinis walked past. I was in awe at their utter lack of concern for how they looked. My fellow beach lovers were clearly happy and content. Not one appeared worried about what others were thinking as they blazed trails in the white sand.

I was not bothered or surprised that bikinis came in so many different shapes and sizes. Actually, the colossal number of carefree, very tan women who dotted the shoreline impressed me, and I wished I could walk among them.

So why couldn't I join their beach brigade? I had been waiting for some unwanted pounds to drop before I felt worthy of being seen in a two-piece. As some of the bikini-clad women walked by, I kept whispering to my daughter, "I wouldn't do that." But did it really matter to me what other women looked like in their bikinis? No! So why did I think anyone would care about how I looked?

It eventually occurred to me that I was ashamed of my extra pounds and lack of tone. I suffered with a severe case of self-consciousness. In other words, I struggled with an acute sense of self-awareness, which was exacerbated by my beliefs about my many shortcomings.

My inner critic was negatively influencing my self-image. This inner critic had an image of what I should look like but didn't. My daughter said my biggest problem was still lamenting the disappearance of what I looked like twenty-five years before. Did it make sense to hang onto that?

We all have a mental picture of who we are, how we look, and what our weaknesses might be. This point of view has more to do with how we feel wearing a bikini than the actual shape and size of our body.

I wanted to know how I could soften my harsh viewpoint. I wanted to feel good about myself—to appreciate myself. This didn't mean I no longer wanted to drop those unwanted pounds—because I did. But in the meantime, I decided I needed to change my inner voice from critic to cheerleader.

To begin with, rather than being so preoccupied with my body and its flaws, I needed to give at least equal attention to my attitude as well as my abilities. I needed to appreciate my talents and celebrate my accomplishments.

While we may all have things about ourselves we would like to improve, we also do many things and have many traits deserving of recognition, appreciation, and honor.

Although my mamma taught me to see the good in everyone, I have sometimes forgotten to include myself in that practice. Focusing on the good we see in ourselves gives us encouragement to continue on a progressive path. Our inner cheerleader will point us onward and forward to higher goals and improvements, assuring us that anything is possible.

Criticizing our features and condemning ourselves can trap us in a self-sabotaging pattern. We may become impossible to please and never appreciate the progress we've made. This can lead to an endless cycle of discouragement and dissatisfaction.

"Beauty is in the eye of the beholder," wrote the Irish romantic novelist Margaret Wolfe Hungerford in 1878. This statement has been written in various forms that express much the same meaning dating as far back as third century BC in Greece. No doubt the opinion of what is beautiful is as varied as there are people.

Look at yourself and others, and embrace your distinctive beauty. As we recognize and accept our unique and extraordinary beauty, we'll discover how truly lovely and loveable we really are—regardless of the size of our bikinis.

Look in the mirror and meet the love of your life. Don't allow someone's "You are . . ." criticism to be louder than your "I am . . ." Be committed to who you are. Love yourself. You've understated your beauty long enough.

Before I could reimagine, reinvent, or reignite my life story, I needed to love the heroine of my story—me!

Be your own rescue. I was beginning to learn what this could mean.

Lipstick Pearl

Today is big with possibilities, potential and lipstick colors.

Part Two
Bronze Treasure

19 | Breaking free from routine
22 | Walk among the giants
26 | Is ignorance ever bliss?
29 | Be a trailblazer!

Bronze Treasure
Be honest with yourself

There's something about Bronze Treasure lipstick that makes me feel natural and naked. Buck naked, for me, is about being vulnerably honest and ready to be taught. Plus, it seemed like the most fitting color for a journey that would take me up close and personal with new-to-me natural settings.

From hikes in search of waterfalls and strolls through redwood forests, to drives along the edge of a dormant volcano and a rocky ocean coastline, Bronze Treasure and shades like it—any brownish hue, really—are shades that won't distract you from embracing your surroundings and discovering a new truth.

How often are you honest with the person who matters most—yourself? I never thought I was lying when I gobbled down a Krispy Kreme doughnut or a yummy bakery item from Starbucks on my way home from running errands, yet still making sure to dispose of the ticket or sack so my husband or daughter didn't find them in my car. It turns out the hiding of my little truths had been a practice I began in childhood when I found ways to hide my candy wrappers so my mamma wouldn't know I had eaten before supper.

Self-deception can take many forms and be motivated by many reasons. For me, my lies usually had to do with food, especially sweets. But self-deception can also be a means to avoid dealing with regrets or keep us from facing our fears of making the changes that would make us happy and satisfied.

Being honest with ourselves destroys our biggest obstacle to living a fulfilling life. Honesty enables us to acknowledge who we are and gives us the strength and opportunity to make changes.

So coat your lips with some Bronze Treasure and put on your most teachable self.

Breaking free from routine

My husband and I finally did it. We finally went somewhere other than Disney World or the beach. All through our daughter's growing-up years, we spent most family vacations going to the places our daughter loved most—and those usually involved Mickey.

Routines are easy to fall into—and they can trap us. Many people have a tendency to do the same things every day, day in and day out. We get up, go to work, come home, fix dinner, eat, do chores, watch television, and go to bed, only to begin our routine again the next day. We feel comfortable traveling within our own little comfort zone, surrounding ourselves with what is familiar.

Our vacations had become routine—like the rest of our life. That is, until our trip to Oregon. My husband was invited to go fly-fishing for the first time with a friend who had moved there. While he went on a two-night camping and fishing trip, I stayed at our rented condo alone and went on daily trail hikes in the nearby hills. Both were things I had never done before.

Our entire Oregon trip was filled with such things—activities new to us that we had never imagined. We crossed mountains, traversed canyons, and hiked trails. We saw the deepest lake, crossed the highest bridge, visited the largest sea cave, saw the most photographed lighthouse, the tallest waterfall, and the oldest and biggest trees, and traveled the windiest roads, rockiest coastline, and the highest and most narrow road of our lives.

Phrases like "branch out" and "stretch yourself" suddenly had fresh meaning. Lyrics written by Tim Rice for Elton John's famous song "Circle of Life" also had new meaning: "There's more to see than can ever be seen / More to do than can ever be done / . . . More to find than can ever be found." Doing things I never thought I could or would had me hungry to experience more.

There's a valuable intuition to be gathered when hiking the longest trail you've ever hiked. I finally understood that it truly wasn't about the destination as much as it was the journey. Although the destination may be worthy and of value, the journey is even more incredible and fulfilling in and of itself. Each moment walking the trails included inspiring vistas and discoveries I would not have wanted to miss, even if I never reached the trail end.

Comfort zones are self-created and imposed. In designing these comfortable and reliable pathways, we tend to limit our possibility and readiness for new experiences.

Stretching is powerful, healing, and transforming. Our Oregon vacation stretched my view of myself from a woman of limited abilities to a woman with unlimited potential.

Being willing to challenge myself to move out of my familiar beliefs and to fearlessly approach new opportunities resulted in a broadened concept of my life. I was ready to welcome more choices, discoveries, and adventures into my life journey. I looked through a fresh lens to see what I could do that is untouched, undimmed, and unimpressed by any beliefs and opinions about age.

Are you trying to find a way out of a mundane routine? Do you feel stuck in a rut and can't figure out what is holding you back?

Branch out and stretch yourself by doing something—anything—you wouldn't ordinarily do. I guarantee you will be glad you did. It's just that simple! Every time you stretch, you enlarge your comfort zone to include more of the great big world out there waiting to be explored. You let go of old, limiting beliefs that had been holding you back from seeing your worth. And, some sparkling, glimmering lipstick may motivate you to get your move on!

Walk among the giants

My husband and I were hiking through a redwood forest—an incredible experience that I highly recommend. It was a bright sunny summer day, although you couldn't tell it as we trekked through a forest so dense it allowed only a trickle of sunlight to peer in.

We came to a section of the forest where many of the big trees were hollow. In fact, I took a picture of my husband standing inside one of these trees. This tree was so big in its hollow center that I suspect a dozen or more people could have stood beside him.

We met a local resident who was also enjoying a hike on this beautiful day, and we asked him about the trees. We were told that a forest fire had hollowed them out. I would never have guessed these huge, healthy trees had ever encountered anything destructive.

This man knew quite a bit about redwoods as he explained the trees had a tough exterior that was almost impenetrable to fire. He said they were so tough that even if only a small part remains alive after a fire, the tree still flourishes and grows. In fact, even when a tree dies, it reproduces itself with seedlings that sprout and grow around its remains.

We learned that although the roots of the redwood are not particularly deep, they are intertwined with their fellow redwoods. Since the trees grow in groves, their roots crisscross each other and form a pattern of support that gives them additional life-giving strength and endurance.

Our new friend told us these ancient trees are equally resistant to insects and disease, which also contributes to their long life span. The giant redwood—or sequoia—is by far the largest living thing on land. And he told us the species had been on earth over 110 million years. Some alive today have lived as long as two millennia. He said this enduring giant whose ancestors stood among the dinosaurs was among the few to survive mass extinction 65 million years ago.

With such hardiness, why is it that only 10 percent of the tree species remain on earth today? Apparently, the greatest and perhaps the deadliest enemy to the redwood has been man cutting them down.

We were intrigued to learn about these inspiring trees. One can't be in their immense presence without being humbled and awed. Isn't there something to be discerned from a life that is far older than us and one that has endured so many hardships?

When I told our daughter about them, she reminded me of a song we heard several years ago at Epcot's World Showcase in Walt Disney World. The song was titled, "We Go On" (music by Gavin Greenaway, lyrics by Don Dorsey, sung by Kellie Coffey), and it played at the close of the evening fireworks show at that time. As I became reacquainted with the song's lyrics, I could see why my story about the redwoods reminded her of this song.

"We go on to the joy and through the tears / We go on to discover new frontiers / Moving on with the current of the years," proclaims the chorus. Certainly when I think of the redwood trees surviving a forest fire, they did continue to "go on" despite what could have been devastating and life-threatening circumstances. These trees have the invincible ability to hold onto the promise of life—a life that expects progress, growth, and to never end.

The lyrics explain how we go on. We go on by "moving forward." How is it we're capable of moving forward even after experiencing the most traumatic day of our life? The song says we keep "moving on" because we have "a spirit born to run."

I believe womankind is instilled with the energizing and uplifting spirit of life. As we understand more about our true passion and purpose, we will learn that we are just as capable as the redwood tree to overcome even the most challenging ordeal and keep moving forward to each new day. It is our natural instinct to do so.

So like the redwood tree, ladies, you and I will go on. We, too, can go through any troubled times and be untouched, unharmed, untarnished, without blemish, spotless, pure, fresh, intact, perfect. My mamma's life has shown me that a woman can go through divorce, death of husbands, and poverty (among other things) and come out on the other side happy and strong, still finding her passion and living her purpose.

Perhaps the redwoods' interconnected root system gives us women the best clue for our own survival. Women (and men, too, for that matter) are already intertwined with one another. Some people have used the phrase, "It takes a village." I am learning more and more that this is true. Maybe it's not so much a matter of it taking a village as a realization that we are in fact living in a village. We are never alone. We are surrounded by others who have walked or who are now walking down a similar path—even the same path as we are. We discover this when we stop looking down at our own feet (and problems) and look around.

Is ignorance ever bliss?

Perhaps you've heard the expression, "Ignorance is bliss, or "What you don't know won't hurt you." I had never given this much thought until we were driving on a very narrow road on top of a volcano. I wasn't the one doing the driving—my husband was. I was sitting on the passenger side determined not to look out the window at the sheer drop off inches from our tires.

My remedy to allay my fears was quickly applying a second coat of lipstick and holding up the roadmap with my right hand in such a way that I could not see out the window. This kept my gaze fixed on the sure road in front of me. So, in that case, perhaps ignorance was bliss. If I didn't know how close to the edge we were, I wasn't afraid.

The phrase, "Ignorance is bliss" comes from a poem by English poet Thomas Gray titled, "Ode on a Distant Prospect of Eton College." The complete phrase is "Where ignorance is bliss, 'tis folly to be wise."

But is it possible to know too much?

Some equate the innocence of childhood with ignorance. Some wish they could return to their childhood, believing that innocence—or lack of worldly knowledge—is a pleasant alternative to the harsh realities of adulthood. Such a person might feel that growing up has brought too much awareness of the flaws of humanity and that not knowing something would be more comfortable than knowing it.

Although at times in my life I might have agreed with such sentiments, I can't see how ignorance ultimately helps. It seems more like a stick-your-head-in-the-sand approach to a challenge or fear. With our head in the sand, we will never be able to see the solution that could be right in front of us.

Maybe this desire for ignorance stems from not understanding the power and freedom self-knowledge can provide. Consider the many evils the world has seen, many times perpetuated by arrogant ignorance. I don't think that ignorance has led or would ever lead to a more blissful world.

With the hope that self-knowledge could be my best hope for a journey to a reimagined self, I became consumed with a desire to understand myself—who am I, what I want. I learned self-knowledge requires knowing my heart, and knowing my heart requires listening to my heart.

Honesty is needed as we endeavor to understand the depth of our heart and find our life purpose. With this self-knowledge, we can free ourselves from bad habits, bad manners, bad traits and tendencies, and bad attitudes as well as obtain our deepest desires and live our dreams.

Perhaps you're wondering how to let your heart guide you, or maybe you're afraid your heart will not lead you in the right direction.

There is a difference between my head talking and my heart. It turns out reason and logic is not always in agreement with the deepest desires and dreams of my heart. The only way I am truly happy and satisfied is when I listen to what my heart is telling me and I follow my heart's guidance. Some call this following your intuition.

For me, when I listen to my heart, I find calmness and an inner peace. Contrary to what some may believe, following your heart is not an emotional roller-coaster ride. That opinion of your heart is your head talking.

In order to hear my heart, I must quiet my rational (sometimes irrational) mind. Just like my rational mind told me to be afraid driving along the rim of a volcano and blinding myself from that view gave me peace of mind, I can also quiet my rational mind from telling me I'm too old or it's too late by shutting out those silly thoughts. How do you shut them out? Different methods work best for different people.

Some begin with repeating a mantra or a prayer. I calm my mind by taking a walk or listening to soothing or inspirational music. Taking a candlelight bath sometimes does the trick, too. Once I am able to quiet my overworking rational mind, I am able to hear my heart. Yes, ma'am, I find my higher self when listening to my heart, and I definitely want my higher self to guide me on my re-imagination journey.

I think Helen Keller knew this when she wrote, "The best and most beautiful things in the world cannot be seen nor touched, but are felt in the heart."

Your heart is heard in stillness. If bliss is what you're seeking, dear ladies, learn to follow your inner compass. It is your heart, not your head, that knows best.

Be a trailblazer!

In an attempt to make birthdays during my fifth decade more positive and proactive, I decided to think of them as the beginning of new years. Each new year brings an opportunity for renewal, regeneration, restoration, and renovation as well as an opportunity to welcome new colors of lipstick. Of course, with the beginning of a new year come new agendas to implement my many new resolutions.

Many of my resolutions remain the same with better health practices to implement, career goals that I intend to pursue, relationships that I hope to improve, places I want to see, rooms in my house that I plan to reorganize, and debts that simply must get paid off. Now, though, since I crossed the midlife age hurdle, my obsession with the idea of doing and experiencing things I've never done before continues to be at the top of my yearly goals.

This makes me think of the introductory words of each Star Trek episode. Remember those? Both the original and the "next generation" series opened with words about exploring strange new worlds and seeking out new life forms and new civilizations—"to boldly go where no one has gone before."

It's words like "explore" and "new" that captured my imagination. I can certainly see that bold action is often required of a trailblazer.

After my husband and I walked a few trails in Oregon, I was grateful for the efforts and accomplishments made by explorers such as Lewis and Clark. Over 200 years ago, they set out on an amazing expedition where they faced unknown people, harsh conditions, and territory they had never traveled before.

Walking through dense forests, even on a well-established trail, made me consider the courage and vision that must have been needed by early trailblazers in order to imagine what was possible even when their view was blocked at first.

Who could imagine that on the other side of some steep mountains could be a mighty ocean? Or who could imagine that in the middle of a dense forest would be a beautiful waterfall?

When we set out on a new trail in life, we usually have no idea what we will find along our path—much less what we will discover at the end of our journey. Many times we probably have an idea about what we hope to find or experience along the way. But most likely, we can't imagine the many surprises that we'll encounter.

We can run into problems if we try to outline our expectations too much. When we don't see what we think we're going to see at the moment we thought we would, disappointment and discouragement can cause us to miss something unexpected and equally as wonderful as what we had hoped for.

So the lesson here, ladies, is to expect the unexpected and love the experience when you're blessed with it. Keep your sense of wonder! Hearts filled with wonder hunger to be surprised and eagerly anticipate the wonderment of all they will see and experience.

Remember the wonder of your first kiss, your first day of college, your first airplane ride, or the first time you wore lipstick?

Another annual resolution of mine is to find new wonder in the "old" things I do each day. Wonder makes our lives more meaningful and enjoyable. I can see now as a mid-lifer how not having wonder could lead to boredom and cynicism. My desire for something new and exciting has come to include not only those things I've never experienced but also a rediscovery of the wonder in what is already in my life.

Ladies, rekindle your sense of wonder and make each new day more "wonder-full." This will make blazing new trails as well as walking old ones much more fun. I can guarantee you'll add more wonder to your day by adding new lip colors to your regime. It works for me!

When you can't change anything else in your life, change your lipstick.

Part Three
Frozen Rose

36 | A room with a view
38 | Go fishing
41 | What if?
44 | When something old becomes new
46 | Don't miss out

Frozen Rose
Soothe your soul and add spark to romance

Consider this, ladies. It's possible to work, work, work, and not know when to give yourselves the time out you need. You may believe you can't afford a vacation or don't deserve to take one. But your brain needs rest, and so does your heart and soul. Emotional and physical fatigue causes stress and poor choices.

Even short breaks when you allow yourself some time to completely disconnect from your daily routines will allow you time to recharge and rejuvenate. A day of hiking, biking, or fishing enjoying nature and exploring local areas of interest can provide the break you need and fill you with much needed inspiration. You may be surprised how these little breaks make you more receptive, responsive, and ready to tackle your world.

Sometimes the getaways I long for most are the ones in a place that promises to nurture and comfort my weary soul. Wearing Frozen Rose lips can bring out my child-side that wants again to live an uncomplicated, easygoing, and worry-free life.

A room with a view

"All I need is a room with a view," I told my husband as we investigated locations for celebrating our wedding anniversary.

The months leading up to our special day had been filled with one unexpected and unwanted situation after another. Mostly, I longed for a break from all the commotion and wanted time to focus only on my marriage.

As we drove the narrow, winding road up the wooded mountain, I had no doubt that I was headed to a secluded, romantic hideaway. Then, we reached the top, and what would become my very own Tuscan villa for the next three nights came into view. The serene atmosphere that embraced me as I walked to the front door assured me I was right where I needed to be.

The balcony view from our room provided a panorama of sky, hills, trees, and lake. Almost immediately, a broader perspective took shape in my mind, helping me to see beyond challenges and dilemmas waiting at home to be solved. My "time out" had begun!

My time outs from the busyness of life have taken many forms through the years—lying on the beach, fishing in a mountaintop lake, walking around our farm, drinking mochas at Starbucks, or even shutting my eyes for a few moments in the midst of a busy day. Now my time out was sitting on an Oklahoma hillside at Lago Vista Bed and Breakfast. Life felt good—or at least better.

The door shut on any worries and concerns the moment I walked onto our balcony. The wide landscape before my eyes broke the spell that was hypnotizing me into a state of uneasiness. I knew a resurrection of my peace of mind was imminent. I was no longer preoccupied with tomorrow or next week, but focused only on the present moment and the beauty, calm, and love that were with me.

We had a satisfying, delicious breakfast each morning on our Oklahoma hillside as we prepared for our day's activities. But even more invigorating and inspiring was the time my husband and I spent each morning meditating and sharing insights and dreams with each other.

When disappointments, fearful speculations, regrets, complaints, or any of life's miseries or pressures threatens to bury us into a tomb of despair, there is a lighter view that can show us the way up, out, and onward. There is no problem too large or daunting when we open our minds to receive fresh inspiration and guidance. Our certainty and confident resolve will aid us in any situation.

I can't always escape to that "room with a view." Perhaps you can't either. But we can rest assured that a lighter, brighter, higher point of view is available to us. This perspective will give us the strength and ability we need to tackle anything coming our way. We often only need to take a little time out to feel the energy and impulse we're longing for.

Go fishing

Fishing is one of those universal sports and hobbies. In fact, fishing resonates with so many people that fishing metaphors abound.

You may say that you are trying to land a job—and you're casting your line into the big job market. When your relationship ends, your best friend assures you there are plenty of fish in the sea. You may tell a brother to drop you a line. In trying to do something online, you say you hit a snag. You exclaim you got a bite when a business responds to your resume. You're trying to lure and reel in possible buyers for the house you have for sale. Perhaps your mom says your new boyfriend is a good catch. I guess we're people who like to talk fish!

What is it about fishing that is so appealing?

My husband and I went on a trout fishing trip in Colorado. Of course, I went lipstick shopping before we left to find the perfect shade for the trip. I was certain it would be a subtle and calm shade of pink. I must say that few things are more relaxing than sitting beneath an evergreen tree on the bank of a crystal clear mountain lake. This is a great time to wear cinnamon or vanilla scented gloss over your lipstick, too! The stress of everyday life dissipates to the inconsequential detail it really is. There's something about fishing from a quiet shore and breathing serene, fresh Christmas-scented air that clears the mind and soothes the soul.

I was surprised by the intensity of focus that trout fishing required of me. It captured my entire attention as I baited my hook and cast my line into the lake. Spellbound, I gazed into the sunny water waiting for my bopper to move and anticipating the bump of a fish taking my bait.

This was no idle time as my daughter thinks—she's never been mountain lake fishing. There was purpose, vision, determination, and expectation. At the day's end after our catch limit was reached and fish were cleaned and cooked, I was ready to rest up for the next day to do it all again.

Before leaving home for our fishing excursion, I had some trepidation about being in a remote area with little to no phone service and no Internet service. I worried that I would feel disconnected from all that I love. But once I begin fishing, I thought of little else.

This mental state of mind is a far cry from my day-to-day experience when home. My normal day involves lots of multi-tasking and many times where I feel like my attention is scattered or over-extended. It's not easy for anything to get my complete focus. This is sometimes frustrating when I want to give my total attention to the task at hand.

Following that fishing trip, I wondered what it was about fishing that was so all-consuming. I wondered how I could give that kind of focus to other endeavors and interests at home.

Sure, on my mountaintop, there were no interruptions—so there were no other choices than my single task of catching fish. At home there are many decisions and choices to be made that compete for my attention.

But the truth is that regardless of the number of items on our to-do list each day, we can only give one thing—or person—our full attention in any given moment. What a revelation that became for me!

The quality of my projects and time spent with loved ones improved by understanding that each required and deserved my full attention in each moment. It was possible to give my full attention as I took one moment at a time and gave my all to that moment.

Yes, there's something about fishing that allows us to take a time out from thinking about our troubles and big decisions—even when we don't get a bite. Inevitably, a fresh perspective comes into view when I return home after such a break.

So, ladies, focus on one moment of your life at a time—give your whole attention to it. When you feel the need for a break, try fishing and see what new point of view you have when you return.

What if?

How many of your decisions and actions are interrupted or halted by "what if" questions? Perhaps you're like me and feel your life has been outlined too much by this often-daunting, sometimes-paralyzing question.

We went to Disney World in Florida at the time when a tropical storm was stirring in the Atlantic. My husband, who is usually the voice of caution, proposed a "what if" question before we left. "What if the storm hits Florida when we're there? Maybe we should cancel."

But I just couldn't cancel a trip we had planned for many months based on a "what if" synopsis. If we had to cut our trip short at some point, we were capable of adapting our plans to do whatever was necessary at any given moment.

So with my sassy new Disney World lipstick purchased and packed, we went. As it turned out, rain never dampened our activities, and the cloudy days and cooler temperatures were a welcome relief.

There have been many other times when I have labored over the question, "What if I'm making a mistake?" I've agonized over this possibility to the point of becoming paralyzed by fear and consequently accomplishing nothing. This has been true for countless job opportunities that I didn't take—some of which I later regretted not taking.

Certainly when trying to make a decision, we should always consider the consequences of every action, so some "what if" questioning is a good thing. But in the end, we do need to act. I suppose, as with everything in our lives, there is a proper balance between questioning, analyzing, and doing.

Have you ever wanted to know what might have happened if you had taken a different direction, perhaps asking, "What if I had known then what I know now?" This question often leads to one conclusion—regret. Regrets can keep us buried in the past.

"What if" is also one of the tantalizing questions in American history. Historians are often intrigued with contemplating what might have been for many defining moments in our history. They sometimes create, in essence, an alternate history. *What if . . . ?* is even the title of several series published by Marvel Comics that explore "the road not traveled" by its various characters.

However, I'm not really certain what good is accomplished by creating "what if" histories since we can't go back in time and change outcomes. We probably always know best with hindsight.

What does seem more beneficial is imagining "what if" scenarios for the future. I like the idea of being a visionary—a person who has the ability to imagine unbounded possibilities and how to make what at first seems impossible possible.

The most helpful "what if" questioning is when one is dreaming of what to do in one's life. The range of ideas are endless when we picture our future from a "what if" basis without limitations or restrictions.

Perhaps "what if" questions do have their proper place and purpose in our lives—especially when they help mold our decisions into wise and productive steps forward.

My midlife "what if" wonderings include: What if I'm not too old? What if I could do whatever I wanted with the rest of my life? What if I knew I couldn't fail? What would I do if I had no fear?

This kind of "what if" thinking has given me the encouragement to replace uncertainty with the assurance of success. My "can do" attitude is gaining confidence. I'm wearing lipstick shades I never imagined I would or could. Watch out world!

When something old becomes new

My husband and I were on a weekend trip for another wedding anniversary celebration. Although we were going back to a quaint town we had visited many times, we were staying at a new bed and breakfast.

My desire to break free from old habits and to be more open-minded has continued in every area of my life. Perhaps it was this change in perspective, purpose, and lipstick that resulted in a new discovery when we toured the familiar town.

Located on the Cane River, Natchitoches, Louisiana, is renowned as the oldest settlement in the Louisiana Purchase Territory, established in 1714, and is also famous for being the film site of *Steel Magnolias* starring Sally Field and Julia Roberts. I never tire of shopping and dining in the city's historic downtown—it is truly an experience.

One of my husband's favorite shops is the Kaffie Frederick General Mercantile, which is touted as Louisiana's oldest general store. It was in this store where I made my discovery.

As we meandered through its many aisles, I happened to look up when we reached the back section of the store. Much to my surprise, I saw an opening in the ceiling with a sign explaining how "skylights" were original to the architecture and provided helpful lighting when there was no electricity.

Frozen Rose

I had toured this store many times and never noticed either the skylight or the sign. I wondered how I could have missed this unique building feature during previous visits—something that had always been there and yet I had never noticed. The store always has so much interesting merchandise to capture my attention, I simply never had the inclination to look up.

It occurred to me that this is not that unusual. Whether in regard to shops, relationships, or our jobs, many times in our lives so much is placed in front of us—crowding or overwhelming our point of view—that it is difficult to see everything else around us.

Since initiating my goals to slow down, to make moments matter, and to be open for new adventures and experiences, I'm not so conscious of the things that used to consume my focus. Consequently, this may be why I discovered the general store's skylights during this visit—along with many other town features I had never noticed before.

Consider how a baby enters the world without preconceptions. She is curious and alert to everything and everyone. She is eager to learn about and understand everything around her. She is receptive and inquisitive.

Imagine approaching each day like a baby. Each day would be filled with new observations to be made, and you would be excited to welcome each one. You would see life as filled with many insights and treasures waiting to be discovered. You would embrace each day with joy-filled confidence and faith.

My midlife hope is to approach each day with such childlike anticipation—always looking for and expecting to discover and learn something new. Something old can become new, again and again.

Don't miss out

Once, when my daughter and I spent a day enjoying some annual Christmas shopping and eating fried green tomatoes, I realized I had eaten my very first fried green tomato only a couple of years before. This was remarkable because I had spent the first half of my life unwilling to try something new.

Some would say we're prisoners of habit. From the way we think and believe to how we react and behave, we resist changes in the patterns we've built for our lives. From my own experience, not trying something was also habit-forming. But habits can be broken, ladies!

"Old habits die hard," the old adage proclaims. In other words, a belief or way of behaving can take a long time to disappear and is not given up easily. I suspect some smokers unsuccessfully trying to quit would agree with this. However, I have brothers who, after smoking for more than thirty years of their lives, easily stopped once they decided to quit. One brother says he quit smoking on New Year's Eve and never broke his resolution. Breaking an old habit is possible, and it need not be arduous.

I've read that we're set in our ways when it comes to our habits, our tastes, and our preferences. Getting stuck in the status quo has been said to come with age. I wonder when we lose our taste for the new.

When it comes to music, I've read that most people are twenty years old or younger when they first hear the popular music they choose to listen to for the rest of their lives. And if you're more than thirty-five years old when a style of popular music is introduced, there's a greater than 95 percent chance that you'll never choose to listen to it. I may be in that remaining 5 percent, at least on some days. But that said, I still definitely enjoy listening to the music of my high school and college days.

When it comes to food, I don't think I ever had the taste for the new, even when I was young. My unwillingness to try new foods became a habit early on.

But, why is repetition so appealing? Some suggest our natural tendency is to revert to deep-rooted memories. Some say we're afraid of making a mistake, failing, or looking foolish. Some believe we acquire patterns of behavior that continue to occur automatically because we don't question or consider a change.

How can we break bad habits and stop misguided reason from directing our behavior? How can we keep our tastes from narrowing and lose our fear of change?

Perhaps we can best begin by not believing a negative label of who we are, such as picky, addicted, obstinate, or unprogressive.

For me, the impulse to try new foods was the result of a reinvented self-image: one with more order, balance, and activity; one that is lighter, happier, and more energized; one that has become more open-minded, spontaneous, and hungry for all things new and different—including food and lipstick.

Take heart, ladies. You need not miss out on the rich, vibrant world out there with its promise for you. Habit and limited thinking need not enslave you! You were born with a nature that is open and receptive to an expansive point of view that is ever new, fresh, and invigorating. If you want to make a change or try something new, like a wild and crazy new shade of lipstick, you can do it.

Opportunities begin with a YES attitude and some kick-ass lipstick.

Part Four
Rick Ruby

54 | Italy—an unexpected spiritual journey
55 | When opportunity knocks
58 | Lighten your load
60 | A world without borders
63 | Give me that mountaintop view
66 | Is balance achievable?
69 | Throw away your to-go cup!
72 | Where the heart is
75 | Because you are somebody special

Rich Ruby

Bring out your courageous self

Who knew wearing this fiery hue could be so life changing? As I was about to set out on some groundbreaking firsts in my life, I felt the need to find some courage. I can't remember how old I was when my lipstick queen mamma instructed me about the amazing power of red. Somehow it was always understood. I have memories of Mamma and her mamma friends sharing secrets with one another with satisfying giggles and winks. But as an adult, I never had the nerve to give it a whirl until I was trying to muster up some courage for an adventure of a lifetime.

If you need to be brave, bold, and daring or you're demanding some respect, red can help you seize the damn day. It will make you sing like Helen Reddy, "I am woman, hear me roar!" You'll feel luxurious, flawless, and passionate. Give your lips a stroke of red and watch your vivacious self appear.

Italy: an unexpected spiritual journey

A trip to Italy would radically change my life—that's why I'm calling it an unexpected spiritual journey. I didn't know it at the time, but I was embarking down a road that would completely alter my perspective.

I don't know why I was so surprised by the dramatic changes to my mindset when I consider the huge hurdles that were overcome for me to take the trip.

My Italian adventure is highlighted in the series of narratives that follow. Before you read them, here's a brief description of me prior to boarding the first leg of my flight to Italy: empty-nest mom, married to same man for thirty years, never been out of the United States, never traveled without my husband, never went on a vacation with only women, never missed my husband's birthday, and primary caregiver of an aging not-very-healthy mother and older brothers.

For me to say "yes" to this trip was huge for me and not my immediate response. But there was something that compelled me to go. I felt I had to go even if I were kicking and screaming all the way. I was emotionally desperate to experience something "new" and "happy." Somehow I knew my life would never be the same—or, that was my great hope!

When opportunity knocks

When opportunity knocks at your door, what do you do? One friend said the answer to this question was obvious: "You open the damn door!"

As a woman who spent much of her life talking herself out of practically everything, I found that opening the door was not so obvious or easy.

I don't believe that opportunities are chance happenings that fall out of the sky into our laps. No, I believe the choices we make and the actions we take move us towards our future. What we choose today has an effect on what happens tomorrow. Our attitude, ladies, has everything to do with our decisions and consequently what opportunities are created.

I finally said "yes" to many opportunities. I'm quite sure it had something to do with me first saying "yes" to red lipstick. My typical answer when someone asked me why I said "yes" was brief and simple—"Why not?"

You have to understand that me saying "hell yes!" involved a big attitude adjustment. I'm the girl who too often over-analyzed and said, "I'm not sure I can, or I don't think I should." Throughout my life, there were many doors that I could have opened but didn't.

For me, the decision to travel internationally for the first time without my husband in the spring of 2010 impacted my life in numerous unforeseen ways. Largely, this included me getting out of my comfort zone to being open to whatever was new and different in just about every way imaginable—including trying new foods and wearing red lipstick. My mamma saved her red lipstick for daring and special occasions in her life. A trip to Italy felt like the time for me to try out the power of red painted on my quivering lips.

It took me a couple of months to accept an invitation to travel to Italy with a friend and stay in a new friend's villa on Lake Garda. During my indecisiveness, whenever I mentioned my opportunity to anyone, the response was, "How can you even consider letting such an opportunity slip through your fingers?"

Keep in mind that opportunities come in many forms. I'm not only talking about travel ones! Sometimes what makes a new opportunity difficult to grapple with is just that—its newness. Perhaps the opportunity is something you've never done or imagined doing. It can seem scary or too difficult to try something new and not feasible to venture into the unknown or unfamiliar.

Let's say you've been saving sky miles for years for the trips you may someday take. Why not use some of those sky miles now? Perhaps you've assumed hotel cost is more than you can afford. But have you done the research to confirm this assumption? Maybe you've diligently saved money for your retirement. Why not spend some of it today instead of saving it all for a tomorrow that may not be there?

There are more opportunities within your reach than you believe. Don't let unfounded assumptions and uninformed fears tell you differently.

Approaching midlife with an "anything is possible" attitude often results in the proof that it indeed is. There are many reasons for expanding your horizons from your tried and true habits and routine.

My willingness to travel beyond the boundaries of my beloved country has broadened my outlook on life's possibilities. Being middle aged has no longer buried the desire to learn and experience new things. I have a fresh appreciation and increased purpose, with a hunger and desire to live life to its fullest.

If you're waiting around for opportunities to knock on your door, my advice is to stop waiting and start making them happen. Opportunities begin with a "yes" attitude, which opens doors and keeps them open, making us ready for anything. When we're ready for anything, the options, the opportunities, and lipstick choices become surprisingly endless.

Have Lipstick, Will Travel

Lighten your load

Saying "yes" was only the beginning! The day had finally arrived. I could hardly believe it. With my courageous red lipstick on, I sat on an airplane soon to be heading on the first leg of my trip—Dallas to Boston. One of the movies I was going to watch in-flight was *Up in the Air*. George Clooney spouted some thought-provoking lines during his "What's in your backpack?" workshop. He explained how "we weigh ourselves down" in many needless ways and then asked the question, "How much does your life weigh?"

The truth is I had felt weighed down with many worries and caregiver responsibilities before my trip. I had to relinquish my self-proclaimed ownership of various responsibilities and any arrogant opinion that I was the only one who could take charge of them. I must admit that while sitting on that airplane, I felt lighter and stronger. I was certain my well-defined red lips were contributing to this new inner strength and freedom.

My wise travel companions had advised me to check only one piece of luggage. It turned out this made for a much easier walk from the parking lot to the lodging in Italy. I soon understood why one suitcase was important. The walk from our car was a long one—and very steep on uneven cobblestones. I'm still amazed at how my inexperienced luggage wheels survived.

It was an incredible feat for me to check one suitcase, however. A lot of downsizing of hair products and precise packing of clothes and shoes was required. I guess anything is indeed possible when one really wants to do something!

Which brings me to another surprising accomplishment that happened while I was in Italy. I bought an exquisite Italian-made purse. The only problem with this lovely item was that it again required some major downsizing. In making the smaller purse switch, I was amazed at how much I was carrying around that wasn't necessary. I was impressed to learn what can be done when I really want to do it.

Who wouldn't want to lighten their load and lead a calmer life? Such was the bigger question that loomed over me as I traveled to and around Italy. Reportedly, over-packing is the biggest travel mistake—as well as a big life mistake. Our life need not be backbreaking. Carrying around unnecessary burdens, fears, and worries—especially those that belong to others—can throw us off balance. The main point for me was realizing how much is unnecessary, pointless, serves no good purpose, and accomplishes nothing good for anyone.

I shifted from overwhelmed to having more efficient, productive, peace-filled days. Remarkably enough, others could take care of their own lives perfectly fine without me. Well, at least most of the time!

Ladies, clean out, disencumber, unburden, unload, reduce your backpack, your purse, your wallet—your life—of everything that isn't yours or necessary. You'll be surprised at how much lighter you'll be.

A world without borders

My mamma quoted Bible verses to me all of my life. This may explain why in so many situations still, a Bible verse comes to my mind. It didn't matter what the original context of the verse was or whether or not it made sense for my current circumstances. In fact, it's sometimes been a curious fit.

This happened as I entered the plane for my flight from Boston to Paris. The phrase, "Enlarge the border of thy tent," came to my thought. When I looked it up in a Bible concordance after I returned home, I found the phrase was, "Enlarge the place of thy tent" (Isaiah 54:2). There were other Biblical references that talked about enlarging one's border as well. This included, "the Lord thy God shall enlarge thy border" (Deut. 12:20).

My daughter had given me a journal to take with me to Italy. So as soon as got to my seat, I wrote in my journal: "Enlarge the border of thy tent." I had a feeling that I was going to be learning just what these words meant during my Italian adventure.

Since I was soon to leave the borders of my own country, it was no surprise to me the word "border" came to mind. After all, I had not been able to get that scary truth out of my head for weeks.

Rich Ruby

Not long after I wrote my journal entry, a beautiful woman in Islamic attire sat down next to me. I noticed she had a prayer book, which she continued to reference prior to our departure. Her actions reminded me that I should also pray for everyone's safe journey.

The flight would be a long one from Boston to Paris—my final stop before heading to Verona, Italy. Naturally, we wanted to converse. This proved interesting since my neighbor spoke very little English, and I couldn't speak anything else.

Still, during the long flight, I discovered quite a bit about her. She was a mother of many children. One of her children lived with her sister in Boston. He was finishing his high school years with plans to attend an American college. I gained respect and compassion for her commitment to the well-being of her children and the separation she was enduring as part of that commitment. Suddenly, I was more aware of what we had in common as mothers than any presumed differences. This was pretty big for me, since there was a time when the sight of someone like her would have brought suspicion and fear.

I became certain that it wasn't luck that I received an invitation to go to Italy. It wasn't coincidence that my airplane neighbor was this woman. It wasn't surprising that my flight was taking place on my dear husband's birthday—an occasion I had never missed in our thirty-plus years together. It's funny because even though I was far away from my husband, it felt like he was with me. That may sound corny, but he so fills my heart that it's impossible to feel separated from him. It required me being away from him to recognize this fact.

There is no doubt in my mind that my concept of home was expanded by this trip. I'm in awe at how a person can be in a foreign country and feel at home. But I did! Turns out the world was created without boundaries, borders, or countries. It took me leaving the comfort and familiarity of my own small world to give any thought to what that meant.

When we're faced with a situation that is forcing us to stretch in some unexpected or unknown way—perhaps going through unchartered waters—we don't need to be afraid. Acknowledgement of a divine power along with some confident and daring lipstick can help us travel through and beyond the confines of limited views and narrow opinions. We learn more about a world without borders—the world that was created for all of us to share together.

Give me that mountaintop view

Do you ever feel like your life is nothing but an uphill journey? When I make such a complaint, it's usually because I'm more focused on the climb—particularly each step I'm striving to make—rather than the broadening view surrounding me as I go up.

I had never stood on a mountaintop before my trip to Italy—much less stood on any snow-covered mountain. So when my friend suggested we take a gondola ride to the top of Italian alp Monte Baldo, I said "yes" with some trepidation and quickly recoated my red lips.

I took the easy and fast way up. Most mountains apparently don't have a way to comfortably ride to their top. Mountain climbing usually involves a slow walk and a steady pace, with spots where crawling is appropriate. There are many stops to take a break and rest along the way. Perhaps if I had walked my way to the top of this mountain, I might have been more prepared for how I felt when I got there.

We trudged through the snow to Baldo's scenic point. "Breathtaking" is a good word, and it wasn't a physiological reaction to the high altitude. I wanted to look down at times to make sure my feet were following the narrow path, but it was almost impossible to not constantly look up and outward to the majestic panorama encompassing me.

I had to pause many times—not for rest—but to take in a deep breath of appreciation for the beauty and observe the new vista.

I had no idea there would be an endless array of other mountaintops capturing my gaze—only visible by air or on top of a neighboring mountaintop. The many hillside villages tucked discreetly away between mountains surprised me. I thought, *I never would have known they were here.*

The butterflies and anxiety I felt before boarding the gondola left almost immediately as I stepped foot on the mountain. With every step, I gained an air of calm, confidence, and self-assurance. I didn't need to ski or ride the snow mobile, although those would have been fun to learn and experience. It was enough—at least that day—to just be there.

I was so glad our mountaintop day was at the beginning of my Italian experience. It helped me value what I had accomplished just by getting on the airplane. It set the tone for the rest of my trip—dare I say, for the rest of my life.

One might think that an invitation to stay in a little Italian villa would not cause any hesitation. But for me, it was one of the most difficult decisions of my life.

Somehow, after a life devoted to the care of my husband and only child, I felt unsure about my life's purpose. I lacked the independence to act on my own or the ability to think about what was best for me.

Standing on top of Monte Baldo brought to mind a Bible scripture: "They rose up early in the morning, and gat them up into the top of the mountain, saying, Lo we be here, and will go up into the place which the Lord hath promised" (Numbers 14:40).

Being on that mountaintop assured me that the Creator promises purpose for our lives. Our purpose doesn't reach a conclusion or diminish with age. Sometimes our journey to achieve our purpose is smooth, sometimes rugged. But it is a peak that is obtainable.

Yes, ladies, our life journey is always uphill. We want it to be! We need it to be! As we go up, with a fresh coat of color on our lips, we are guaranteed a wider point of view. We definitely want to reach that ultimate vantage point that the top of the mountain provides. Give me that mountaintop view! It's worth every step to get there.

Is balance achievable?

Balance had long been among my greatest desires. I would try to imagine what balance in my life could look like. I talked about it and I wrote about it. But I never experienced balance until I went to Italy.

With every bite of my Italian cuisine, I experienced the meaning of balance—that perfect blending of flavors. Yes, Italian chefs had definitely mastered it!

Italians use only fresh ingredients—nothing frozen or from a can or jar. Flavor is so much richer when using fresh vegetables, pungent herbs, and whole cheeses. I learned in my Italian cooking class how to make pasta—it's easy! I vowed I would never eat pasta again unless I made it from scratch. I'm not talking about using a pasta machine. We rolled, patted, and cut our dough into perfect pieces. The difference in taste and texture from what I was used to was amazing.

In Italy, each ingredient is equally important to reach the desired flavor. Each ingredient by itself is meaningful, and you can't imagine your recipe without it. No one ingredient overpowers another. There is never too much sauce!

I always know it's a dish I will love when I love every ingredient—even when I've never mixed the ingredients together before. It is also fun to try a new ingredient and discover a new love.

So what does all of this have to do with achieving balance in my life? My new appreciation of how Italian chefs achieve balance in their cooking led me to evaluate the "how" in all aspects of my life.

Had I become stuck in some old routines to the point of not finding satisfaction or joy in what I was doing? Had I become more concerned with how quickly I could accomplish something rather than regarding the quality of the end result? Were there "ingredients" in my day that I genuinely didn't like? Were there things I longed to include but I didn't? Was there any one thing that was demanding all of my time to the exclusion of something else that was important to me?

If you find you can answer "yes" to any of these questions, ladies, like I could, perhaps it's time to make some changes. Making changes was easier than I thought it would be. In fact, it can be as easy as the Nike slogan, "Just do it!"

Remember all those ingredients that you would never leave out because they were needed to achieve the finished product? I thought about the activities that were most important to me and to my day, like talking with my mamma, playing with my sweet dog, going for a walk at sunset, spending time with my husband and daughter, reading, and writing in my journal. I realized the importance of never leaving them out. Why would I ever? It isn't difficult to understand why my days were feeling off-balance when they were missing something I felt was essential to my happiness, peace of mind, and well-being.

We must be honest with ourselves, ladies. This necessitates us truly getting our priorities in the right order. For me, just like trying that new ingredient in a recipe, this included the strong desire to experience things I had never done before or going places I had never been.

Now, I look at anything in my life that has become routine and ask how I can make the old, mundane, or boring fresh and new and interesting. I focus on what's most important to me and make those things my top priority each day—instead of maybe fitting them in, maybe not. No more worrying and fretting about balancing all the other stuff that didn't matter that much. The result has been more happiness and satisfaction. (And maybe a not-so-clean house!)

Who would imagine that a trip to Italy and the enjoyment of its fabulous food could impact your entire life?

After my trip, for the first time in my life, I knew balance was not only possible, but it could be achieved to the utmost perfection—just like that meat sauce I relished in Bologna or the farfalle with veal sauce I savored in Verona. Yum!

Throw away your to-go cup!

Italy must be felt—not merely seen. There are many sights to see, but if you rush around trying to see as many as possible during your visit, you will miss the most important experience of all—cappuccino.

I fell in love with cappuccino while I was in Italy. Perhaps this love affair was possible because cafes do not serve your cappuccino in a to-go cup. No, the only way to truly enjoy a soothing cup of cappuccino is in a small china cup. This requires you to stop, sit, and sip your drink. Sipping your cappuccino while wearing brilliant red lipstick is a powerful combination.

This magical hue smeared onto the rim of my china cup prompted me to focus all the more on how I was feeling as I relished my many cappuccino encounters. I loved how I felt as I slowly savored the taste—not wanting my cup to empty too fast. I felt calm, attentive, refreshed, and happy.

Italian cappuccino and red lipstick taught me what it means to live in the moment. No longer were those just words that sounded like a good idea. Before my trip, putting those words into practice was harder than it sounded.

Even the tour guide in Bologna emphasized the importance of feeling what we were seeing. For instance, in all the churches we visited, she said what was important was to notice how they made us feel—each an example of a distinct architectural style and time in history.

She said, too, that each church represented a different understanding of humanity's relationship to God. One church with its long narrow aisle directed your gaze toward the cross at the end, she said. We could feel a congregant entering with her head down, waiting for a better life after death. Another church had numerous tall windows that filled the sanctuary with light and warmth. A beautiful mural decorated the ceiling. This, she said, enflamed the hope of a better life, possible right now.

One of my friends questioned our tour guide about the name of a church we had just explored. The guide said its name didn't matter. She wanted us to think only about how it made us feel.

Life may not pass us by, ladies, but we can pass life by if we walk too fast. In Italy, I learned to slow down. The learning came as I focused on and appreciated each moment. I took a deep breath with every step, and I couldn't help but walk more slowly.

I remember a line from a favorite country song by the band Alabama: "I'm in a hurry and don't know why." I do know why I'm no longer in a hurry! Living six days in Italy was enough to help me understand.

Life happens in the moments. Each moment is precious and longing to please us, love us, comfort us, and engage with us, if only we slow down and allow ourselves to experience each one. I don't want to ever miss a moment of life again.

To make sure I didn't, I bought everything I needed to make cappuccino when I got home with a moka pot, milk foamer, and Italian espresso. Making and having a delicious cup of cappuccino before I start each day helps me remember what is most important. As much as possible, whether at home or in a coffee shop, I enjoy my cappuccino as it was intended—drinking from a china cup, wearing red lipstick.

Where the Heart is

It's a humbling experience to be dependent on those around you to find your way and make you feel comfortable in unfamiliar surroundings. When I returned to the United States, I became acutely aware of directional signs I had never before noticed, written in several other languages, strategically placed to be of service to the many visitors our country welcomes from every continent of the world.

Since I lived in twelve different places during the first seventeen years of my life, I know what it feels like to be the new kid on the block. During those years, I lived in houses, duplexes, mobile homes, hotels, and a car. I went to seven different schools in three states. But I can attest that no matter where I lived, I felt at home. Perhaps this also helps to explain why—for me—home has never been confined to a location. It also explains how I could feel so at home in a country I had never been to before.

Still, I used to think of home as connected to a person. When I think about my childhood, I could say home was wherever my mamma was. Since marrying my husband, home has been wherever he was. But even though my husband wasn't with me in Italy, I felt completely and comfortably at home. The more I reflected on the way I felt, the more my curiosity was piqued.

Home has been defined in many ways. Some say home is a safe environment—a place where you have no worries or problems, where you feel peace, where you love to be, where you feel comfortable and content. Some say home is with a certain person or in a place you love most. But is home dependent upon person or place? My Italian experience told me it wasn't.

It has been written, "Home is where the heart is." Trying to understand exactly where my heart was could be the reason I went to Italy. This searching of my heart was not something new. It began when my only child left for college. But as the years passed, my searching continued. Prior to my trip to Italy, my search had become more urgent.

Much has been written for those searching their heart. Some informative quotes include, "As he thinketh in his heart, so is he" (Proverbs 23:7). "Where your treasure is, there will your heart be also" (Matthew 6:21). But one of the most compelling ideas I've come across is one by author Mary Baker Eddy: "We should examine ourselves, and learn what is the affection and purpose of the heart, for in this way only can we learn what we honestly are."

For the first half of my life, who I was seemed simple—I was a daughter, a sister, a college student, a wife, a teacher, and a mother. But I now wondered if this was enough for my life. I questioned if I had been defining myself correctly.

Perhaps who I am had nothing to do with what I had done or how others saw me, but everything to do with my own heart—my perception and understanding of who I was and the purpose for my life.

Because my trip to Italy felt spiritually directed, I felt a divine presence while I was there. I was in a constant state of examining my heart and listening for what I would be told. Divine truth and love had much to say about who I was and my purpose. I took to heart every inspiration that came. When I asked, "Why am I here?" a voice said, "Because you are needed." When I cried, "I feel lost," a voice said, "You're where you are supposed to be." When I questioned, "What do I do next?" a voice suggested, "Try something you've never done before."

During my trip to Italy, I came to the conclusion that home is where God is. Guess what? "There is no spot where God is not!" This fun spiritual idea first entered my life by way of my daughter's Sunday School class. I've remembered it ever since.

This is why I felt at home when I was in Italy, even while separated from the people and places most beloved and familiar to me. This is why we can all feel the divine presence any time and anywhere. For where our heart is, so is the Divine—loving us, encouraging us, comforting us, and guiding us.

Rich Ruby

Because you are somebody special

After my return home from Italy, my husband and I began enjoying a delicious breakfast routine. One of our favorite combinations includes French toast, fresh fruit, and a yummy cup of cappuccino. Breakfast is not only great tasting but also a lovely beginning for each new day.

In Italy, food was delicious and served like a masterpiece painting on a plate. Since my return—especially at breakfast time—I get immense pleasure in arranging the food on our plates in some exquisite way. It's amazing how taking the time to do this simple yet thoughtful gesture makes us enjoy our meal all the more, as well as setting the tone for a happy and satisfying day.

One morning when my husband took his dad to have breakfast with some of his friends, I thought, *Why shouldn't I still fix myself a beautiful breakfast?* I took the time to make my plate as lovely as I did when I was serving both of us.

As I sat down to eat alone, I observed what I had done. My napkin and silverware were neatly in place on the table, and the arrangement of food on my plate and cappuccino served in an elegant cup and saucer were picture perfect. I thought, *What a special breakfast I'm about to give myself. And why not?*

Because I'm "precious in his sight" were the words that came to mind. My mamma taught a song in my childhood: "Jesus loves the little children / All the children of the world / Red and yellow, black and white / They're precious in his sight / Jesus loves the little children of the world."

And this, ladies, is also the reason you should do the same. You, too, are precious in his sight. In other words, you are somebody special!

Believing in our innate value and treating ourselves with care is imperative. If we don't, we might be tempted to think we don't matter, that our life doesn't make a difference or is insignificant. These lies would fool us into believing we are not worthy, not good enough, or not capable enough. None of which is true, by the way!

You are special because you're you. Being different from one another is what makes each of us special. We all have unique gifts and talents. We can be who we are meant to be—ourselves.

Being special—or being ourselves—means we are exceptional, important, significant, unique, extraordinary, and memorable. We have a quality, character, and identity that are distinguishable from everyone else. I believe that each of us has been especially designed for a particular purpose. So, ladies, each of us matters.

Many years ago I read a quote by Mother Teresa: "We ourselves feel that what we are doing is just a drop in the ocean. But if that drop was not in the ocean, I think the ocean would be less because of that missing drop." This quote reminds me that my life does matter and is important in my world. This thought has inspired and encouraged me all the more to reach my full potential—that it's necessary and imperative that I do.

Give yourself permission to be yourself. Don't allow yourself, or anyone else, to limit your possibilities—or your lipsticks—by saying what you should or should not do or what you can or cannot do. You must be you and whatever that entails.

Do what you love! If you love to write, then write. If you love to sing, then sing. If you love to farm, then farm. If you love to teach, then teach. There is a way to be whoever you aspire to be.

Being yourself can require some nurturing and tender, loving care. I have found it important to invest in my physical and emotional self each day. This includes blocking out time to ponder what is important to me and to consider how precious I am in my mamma's (and God's) eyes.

Enjoying your own company by fixing yourself a fabulous meal and serving yourself with elegant stemware is another way to treat yourself with tender loving care. Why should you do this? Because you are somebody special!

Lipstick Pearl

It's never too late to try a new shade of lipstick... among other things.

Part Five
Fuchsia Fever

83 | Why not seize the moment?
87 | Someday is now
90 | Resolve to keep your heart young
93 | When simple is not so simple
96 | Be a possibility thinker

Fuchsia Fever
Boost your determination and confidence

Perhaps it's time for you to ask, "What have I been waiting for? Some fuschia fever on your lips may embolden you, like it did me, to see that there is no reason to wait. The someday you've been waiting for is right now!

That's right! For me, there was no more waiting to lose weight, to begin an exercise program, to go blonde, or to be happy—no more waiting for the so-called perfect time and place to enjoy my life. Yes, I finally decided there would be no more delay in being honest with myself. I took on that huge question, "What in the hell do I want to do next in my life?"

That's the long and short of it—a simple decision to take action and to take action now. All of these actions resulted not so much in a new me, although it may appear that way on the outside to many. It was more of a discovery of the woman I was born to be.

You must fall in love with yourself enough to honor yourself. Don't wait to find time for yourself—you have to make the time. Look in the mirror, ladies, and see the miracle that you are. Coat your gorgeous lips with some luscious lipstick. Remember you are beautiful, strong, fun, interesting, intelligent, hopeful, brave, and confident. You have passion and purpose. Always and forever—with or without lipstick!

Why not seize the moment?

My husband long had fishing in Alaska on his bucket list. Since I had never fished there and I was now dedicated to a life of anything new, I was ready to go. Of course, I decided I could use some new lip color for the trip—something that helped me get ready for what I was certain could be a trip of a lifetime. My new spunky fuschia fever lipstick didn't disappoint.

I felt playful, passionate, and filled with love of life as we embarked on our journey. This was a good thing, since our Alaskan adventure would include fishing for halibut in extreme wind and wave conditions and king salmon river-fishing in bear country. I do mean lots of close encounters with bears! Our guide told us if any bear came toward us, to simply slowly retreat to the riverbanks and let the bear fish where he wanted. Easy to follow advice! Oh, and I should add we flew in a small float airplane to go river fishing in bear country. I used an entire tube of lipstick during that trip!

I should brag how I was one of two women among several men at the fishing camp and I caught the biggest king salmon and halibut. I was also not the one who got seasick! Just saying.

Another trip that was on my husband's bucket list was a trip to Switzerland. I had already been to Switzerland once with one of my dearest girlfriends—another trip to Europe without husbands, a few months after my Italy trip. My just-girls trip also included going to Austria and meeting up with my friend's daughter when she was on-the-job in Germany. My favorite memories from my first trip to Switzerland included seeing the Christmas tree lighting in Salzburg, the incredible holiday street decorations in Vienna, and drinking lots of yummy cappuccino and eating hot crescents with strawberry jam on our train rides.

I couldn't wait to go back to Switzerland with my husband, who has been a train lover since boyhood. We made a big track around the country during our ten-day anniversary celebration. My spunky hot pink lipstick came in handy as our train made the Glacier Express trek. We both especially loved the castles in Bellinzona and touring the Chateau de Chillon in Geneva.

But it was during the months leading up to these trips when epiphanies, such as "someday is now," occurred that taught us that we could no longer wait to seize the moment and fulfill some of our life dreams and travels.

When we were still stuck in neutral and perhaps looking for permission to move forward, I asked several of our friends what their reasons were for not seizing moments in their lives. Hearing their excuses helped me and my husband realize we could no longer do the same.

Fear was high on the list of reasons for many folks—fear of what may happen, fear of failure, fear of change, fear of risk. Some said uncertainty about a decision—questioning if it's the best thing to do or not—generally makes them afraid to act and so they don't.

Plain ole procrastination was the reason for some. Sometimes we put off seizing moments because of laziness. We hesitate to make a decision, so we put off thinking about it, only to figure out later what should have been done or said.

Fretting over time rather than living in the eternal now keeps many from seizing the moment. In what I call the "Scarlet O'Hara" approach we say, "Maybe tomorrow would be a better time," but when tomorrow comes, it is too late. The moment, the opportunity, the possibility, is "gone with the wind."

Time excuses can also stem from stubbornness and rigidity or even indifference and inertia. As one friend put it, "My schedule is already too full, or there are already too many demands on my time. It's easy to get so involved in the present moments that cry for my attention, that I can fail to perceive a special opportunity to help someone."

Sometimes it's a matter of "my way" or "no way." One friend said, "I had other plans at the time and didn't want to change my plans." I'm not saying changing our plans is always the thing to do in every situation, mind you, but still, perhaps it's good to be flexible and spontaneous so we leave some room for moments that could be seized.

How we view ourselves can greatly impact whether or not we seize moments. One friend said sometimes he looks at his limitations and lets this view determine what he can do, think, or appreciate. Such a view always makes us believe we don't have the ability needed. Or we may just feel unworthy. Guilt often turns into an attitude of unworthiness.

Sometimes to seize or not to seize the moment becomes a battle of wills—human will or the divine. A friend said, "Maybe you know it's right to do something, but you don't let yourself. You let some reason sway you in a different direction."

Many people live their days so mired in the past or worried about the future that they remain unaware of the treasure of the present that they already possess. We can waste precious time worrying about some future moment. What has often happened to me in the past is that I would worry about something that could happen. Then circumstances changed and whatever I was concerned about doesn't even exist anymore. Priceless moments, which could have been savored, were lost.

This reminds me of the song by Seals & Crofts, "We May Never Pass This Way Again." One stanza encourages us to "Sail our ships out on the open seas / Cast away our fears and / All the years that come and go." Yes, ladies, enjoy each moment before it passes you by.

My husband and I decided to take more time to enjoy life and to stop putting our dreams on hold. Thus our trips to Alaska and Switzerland.

Now when we go on any short or long vacation, we're committed to being on vacation and not thinking about work and other worries waiting for us when we get home.

Savoring each moment of our lives brings joy and thankfulness. I want to be willing to explore new territories, go places I've never been. Life is fresh, exhilarating, and full of hope and open windows when we live fully and mindfully in the moment.

Someday is now

Some years ago I bought a Curly Girl Design greeting card that remains on my desk. The phrase on its cover is one that I read every day: "One of the hardest things to realize," the card's character says, "is that someday is right now."

I recall one of those "someday" moments when my husband and I went to a movie. (I say "someday" because usually when we talk about wanting to go see a certain movie, we never end up going to see it.) Interestingly enough, a character in the movie spoke to this very point. Tom Cruise says, "Someday. That's a dangerous word. It's really just a code for 'never'" *(Knight and Day)*. People often speak of the things they will never do.

I don't want this to be me! Are you with me, ladies?

I've been carrying around another quote from a Curly Girl Design notepad page. By a fun image of a female character, it reads, "The world is full of people who will go their whole lives and not actually live one day. She did not intend on being one of them."

This little piece of paper is tucked neatly away in my wallet so that I come across it frequently. It reminds me that I don't intend to be one of those women who never lives her own life, but rather a woman who finds her own dreams, goals, passion, purpose.

I used to say that I felt like I was living from one vacation to the next. I won't stop planning vacations—and as many as possible, too. But I decided that I also needed to value each day in between and give more consideration to the promise that each day had to offer.

I remember being a starry-eyed teenager who spent many hours and days dreaming about someone, someday, and somewhere. I wonder if I missed something while I was busy gazing off to some distant horizon.

How can people go their whole lives and not actually live, anyway? What does this mean? One dictionary defines "those who truly live" as those who "enjoy life to the full"—as those who "pursue a positive, satisfying existence."

It's possible to go through the motions of what's expected each day and not be fully engaged in each moment. If we're not fully engaged as active participants in the day, we are not being aware and appreciative of all there is to enjoy. Thus, we're not living the day.

It's no wonder we can find ourselves dissatisfied with our lives. If we think that satisfaction or joy is dependent upon someday or somewhere in the future, we limit the satisfaction and joy we can experience right now. It can become impossible for us to be satisfied and happy.

There was a time when I was worried that my life would reach its final chapter before all of my somedays could come to fruition and all my somewheres could be visited. This was also during the time when I had forgotten there were still hundreds of lipstick colors to discover.

I decided that I needed to be more appreciative of what I had already accomplished and experienced up to that point. I don't think I was valuing my life enough. Gratitude has a way of reminding us of all that's good in our lives.

Because I was concentrating on all the somedays and somewheres I had not seen yet, I neglected to appreciate all the ones that I had.

Do you have a someday—or a someone or somewhere—you're looking forward to?

Asking myself this question is exactly how I began my weight-loss journey. Years of buying and loving Blue Bell ice cream (3 gallons for $10) resulted in at least 35 pounds of excess body weight. Well, that's the excuse I've used through the years, anyway! For years, I promised myself I would go on a diet and drop the unwanted pounds.

Once I concluded my someday was right now, I made a phone call to a personal trainer who had been recommended to me. Monica's business was called "Way Out Wellness," which was so fitting for where I was living. Living "way out" in the country on a cattle ranch, at least an hour from fitness facilities in a city, I was excited to find a trainer to help me get going with my "someday" not only right now, but right where I was.

I made the commitment to work with my trainer twice a week. But it would take a daily lifestyle change to accomplish my weight loss goals. Daily walks and eating clean and lean were added to my "someday is now" agenda. Six months later not only were my goals reached but my clothes size was cut in half, from size 12 to size 6.

Let me repeat the question: Do you have a someday—or a someone or somewhere—you're looking forward to?

One thing is certain. If we look only to something in the future, we will miss something in our present. Don't miss the joy of this day and every day, ladies. Life really is what we make it, so let's make it the best one possible, one day at a time. We can make our someday right now.

Resolve to keep your heart young

I was listening to a Frank Sinatra CD when his song, "Young at Heart" caught my attention. I had heard it sung many times and had even seen his 1954 movie with the same title, co-starring Doris Day.

His song gives some assurances that come with being young at heart, such as fairy tales can come true, life gets more exciting with each passing day, it's hard to be narrow of mind, and you can laugh when your dreams fall apart at the seams. All of these things are possible, Frank sang, when we're young at heart.

His song suggested that being carefree and happy isn't based upon age. I suspect many of us fondly recall—and some of us long for—our youthful days of less responsibility and more energy. But according to Ol' Blue Eyes, it sounds like an ageless lifestyle is grounded by an eternally youthful outlook. A youthful outlook isn't only in spite of one's age, but also in spite of one's circumstances and experiences.

American baseball player Satchel Paige, also renowned for his philosophy on staying young, asked a poignant question. He proposed, "How old would you be if you didn't know how old you were?"

It could be that too much awareness of our age develops into an excuse. Whether that excuse seems very real or it is imagined or assumed, age becomes the basis for our limitations, inabilities, inactions, boundaries, obstacles, and confinements. I have wondered how my thoughts as well as my actions, decisions, and dreams would change if I dismissed completely any thought of getting old or older.

Since entering so-called middle age, there's a long list of synonyms for old that I want no part of. Synonyms like obsolete, antiquated, outdated, dull, worn out, and most importantly—gray-headed. That will never happen to this girlie!

On that note, here's how I went from a short-haired brunette to a long-haired blonde.

I was born a brunette with lots of thick, very straight hair. In fact, I had so much hair, my mamma and Aunt Dot gave me a Toni Permanent when I was only six months old while I sat in the kitchen sink.

My mamma wanted curly long hair for her little southern belle baby. Did I tell you I was born in Atlanta, Georgia, in the 1950s? I had gorgeous long hair much of my early childhood. My short hair began when I made Junior High Drill Team in Dallas, Texas, and chin-length hair was a requirement for all the girls on the squad. Never again was my hair as long as it was when I was five—until now.

It turns out my hair is not turning grey, but is white like my maternal grandmother. After a few years of coloring various shades of brown and red, my hairdresser suggested blonde highlights as a way to disguise my white roots. Before we resolved to change the color, I had let my hair grow. Maybe it was wearing a size 6 again—something I had not worn in thirty-plus years—that was helping me to see myself as younger rather than older. My new body seemed to require new hair on top of it. The longer my hair got, the blonder we colored.

Sometimes big changes require bold decisions!

It's all good fun to me. My approach to decisions like this is, "Why not?" If I don't find a good enough reason not to, I say "yes!"

Perhaps staying young and maintaining a youthful point of view is possible and for the most part within our control.

Why can the young at heart laugh when their dreams fall apart? Because the young at heart are visionaries!

If one dream doesn't turn out like they dreamed, they envision a new dream—a new possibility, a new path, a new opportunity. As I recall my own childhood memories, I don't think a day went by without me dreaming about my future. That future was filled with numerous ideas and options—many of which are still attainable and many of which I've not yet pursued. What am I waiting for?

The young at heart know no limitations, boundaries, or obstacles. They only envision or imagine what is possible. They are flexible, adaptable, and buoyant. They don't take matters so seriously. They have the innate ability to lighten up absolutely everything they encounter. Consequently, they are able to lessen the oppressiveness or severity of any situation and make the changes needed to reach their goal.

So ladies, may we all cast away our old-age blinders and return to that childhood vision —where we see only the infinite. Surely this is how we keep our heart young. This point of view will lead us to our own bottomless drawer for possibilities and lipstick and hair colors.

When simple is not so simple

When searching for a way to de-stress and simplify my life, a trip to the beach is usually my ultimate solution. Of course, if the trip right at that moment isn't possible, I must find solutions right where I am.

A statement in an article caught my attention: "In a world of overwhelming choice, technological complexity and diminishing free time, consumers are desperate to simplify their lives" (Rob Tannen, director of research at Bresslergroup, a U.S. product design consultancy). His words "desperate to simplify" could definitely describe middle age me!

The article is actually titled after a favorite acronym of mine: "Keep it simple, stupid," or K—I—S—S. Whether to you this means the above or "Keep it short and simple" or "Keep it short and sweet," its meaning is obviously focused on whatever simple entails—uncomplicated, effortless, manageable, and fundamental. I must say that simple does sound like a wonderful way to do things!

Some say the KISS method or principle has its basis in various statements in history, such as Albert Einstein's, "Everything should be made as simple as possible, but not simpler." Or Leonardo da Vinci's, "Simplicity is the ultimate sophistication."

The Dalai Lama once said that simplicity is the key to happiness in the modern world, and yet for many of us, simplicity feels like the impossible dream. Confucius said, "Life is really simple, but we insist on making it complicated."

It has certainly never been my intent to make my life complicated. I asked my husband why he thought it was so difficult for life to be simple. He said, "People have too many commitments and responsibilities. The demands on our time are too consuming."

It can seem impossible to shorten our list of commitments. Perhaps we see no way to pare it down. What can we do?

Ladies, I wish I could say I've figured out the simple solution to this not-so-simple question, but I haven't. I try now to remember all the simple things that have made my life so sweet. What has brought me the most profound joy are the most simple of things.

When I was a child, simple joys would have been blowing dandelions, making flower necklaces, looking for a four-leaf clover (which required hours sitting in a field of clover), watching clouds and imagining what their shapes looked like, walking barefoot in the grass, watching for falling stars, and of course, trying out my mamma's lipstick colors. Most of these are still on my adult "what makes me happy" list!

I would also now add things like listening to the sound of ocean waves, smelling evergreen trees and fresh cut hay, going for a walk at dusk, savoring my favorite dessert or a cup of cappuccino, and relishing the kiss and hug from a loved one.

The more I think about all the things that bring me joy—and peace of mind—the more I believe that happiness isn't dependent upon the minutia of the day-to-day. The pleasure in the simple is found in our active appreciation of the present. Living in the now tells us there are no ordinary moments. Each moment of our life is extraordinary.

Downsizing, de-cluttering, and prioritizing are all well and good and can certainly be helpful. Trying to maintain some sense of balance in one's life is good, too. But I've decided to add making sure each day includes at least one of the simple joys that have always brought me happiness—while wearing a favorite lipstick, of course. Something tells me that these are all steps in simplifying life right now, right where I am.

Be a possibility thinker

Have you ever considered yourself to be like Leonardo? Yes, the famous Italian Renaissance artist and inventor Leonardo da Vinci. Being like Leonardo means you're on a life-long quest to find answers to all of your questions.

Do you believe dreams can be turned into realities? Do you, like Leonardo, believe anything is possible? At any age? In other words, are you a possibility thinker?

Have you ever asked yourself, "Where's that childlike spirit with that unstoppable and boundless curiosity?" I don't think it's lost. It's just been covered up with the rigidity and perhaps comfort of routine. Fear of failure sometimes holds us back from trying something new, or fear of change, or fear of the unknown.

I'm reminded of an old saying—"Whether you think you can, or think you can't, you're probably right." Remember that scene from the 1980 Star Wars movie, *The Empire Strikes Back?* When asked to raise his sunken star fighter from the Dagobah swamps, Luke Skywalker responded he would try. "No," scolded Yoda. "Do or do not. There is no try." But Luke was not certain the Force could lift such a massive object. And indeed, he failed.

Yet Yoda, using the Force, did lift the fighter and place it on dry land. Luke exclaimed, "I don't believe it." Yoda replied, "That is why you fail."

The power of possibility thinking is becoming clearer in my middle age. A possibility thinker is one who has faith that anything truly is possible—who doesn't let fear of failure stop them from taking action or from trying something new.

A possibility thinker dares to imagine and reimagine again and again. She doesn't let perceived limitations about age stand in her way. She doesn't allow past failures to halt present actions. She doesn't view failures as mistakes but rather lessons revealed. She continues moving forward on her life journey. She never gets stuck in idle and overcome with regrets.

A possibility thinker is persistent, confident, determined, and optimistic. She doesn't let discouragement take hold. She enjoys new challenges. She has faith that there is a solution—and that she need only be committed to its pursuit.

Leonardo da Vinci was clearly a possibility thinker. He imagined the possibility of flying machines, armored tanks, shoes that could walk on water (later known as skis), and plastic—centuries before these prospects became realities. He never gave up his search for solutions, and he never stopped trying to make his dreams into realities. His desire to learn was tireless and endless. Failures merely told him to take a new approach.

I may not know everything the future holds for me, but I'm ready to put fears of uncertainty and age behind me to make new choices and embark on new adventures. I'm quite certain this will involve much more travel and many more lipstick colors!

After my first decade of empty nest travels and learning, I've reached this certain conclusion. Purpose in life never reaches some grand finale. It may change over time or it may look different than you imagined it would, but there is a purpose with all of its implications and possibilities to be experienced. Stay open and flexible, dear ones, and be willing to reimagine your life, making adjustments and changes as necessary. You'll find the satisfaction you long for at every stage of your life.

Join the Have Lipstick, Will Travel Facebook group!

Have Lipstick, Will Travel Facebook Group

It's amazing and powerful how never-before-worn lipstick color can inspire you to think and act differently. Below I feature some great women sharing their early memories of lipstick. I want to hear from you, too! So I'm thrilled to let you know about the Have Lipstick, Will Travel Facebook group, an online community for friendship, encouragement, and camaraderie.

Women can both celebrate their triumphs and get support through their struggles. The fun part is its members are best at coping with challenges, conquering fears, and changing their world when wearing lipstick.

Women helping women is at the heart of the mission of my book and the Facebook group. I hope you will go to the Facebook group page to share your life-changing news with other like-minded women. I look forward to seeing you there!

My grandmother was an Avon lady, too. She had lots of samples lying around—and I sure did love to try on lipstick. My grandmother always wore bright red lipstick and even when she was just cleaning house. It was her way. If I ever saw her without her red lipstick (which was almost never), she just didn't look like my grandmother. She was an independent little thing. I just loved her. Every now and then I'm blessed to have her in a dream. I don't remember, but I'm sure the lipstick is there too. Thanks for reminding me of my grandmother.

By the way, I also feel quite nakey without my lippy stick!

—Frances S., Camarillo, California

My mom was not in favor of me wearing any kind of makeup/lipstick when I was in grade school. She used to buy Avon and had many of those little sample lipsticks around. I, and many other little girls, used to take these to school and put the lipstick on in the restroom. We would reapply often during the day (feeling so grown up); however, at the end of the school day you would find us in the bathroom scrubbing the stuff off before we walked home. I'm sure we had our moms fooled!

—Barbara L., Skiatook, Oklahoma

My beautiful mama definitely wore lipstick, and my sisters and I loved to play in her makeup. Her spirit was bold and blissful. I guess that rippled down to us girls as well. Wearing lipstick or lipgloss can express a playful and colorful spirit. If we play boldly, we can live boldly! Then we can be that kid that knew anything is possible. We can find our edges and our aha moments, our moments of stillness and our glimpses of "I can do anything." We can make OURSELVES proud, not just our mamas. Although we know they are and always will be. Get out there and be the most fabulous you!

—Mia K., Boston, Massachusetts

Remember Yardley's Slickers? There was actually a commercial with a song, "Slicker under, Slicker over, Slicker alone." My first lipstick was a set of about ten Slickers in a box. I'll never forget the thrill of having so many beautiful pastel colors to wear. I keep something like a Slicker in my car all the time still, to put on when going to gym, shopping, etc."

—Judith T., New Holland, Pennsylvania

There was a lady at our church who sold Avon, and of course, my mother was a regular customer. I loved to look through those little catalogs! The little lipstick samples were my favorite things. My mother used to give them to me. I practiced putting on the lipstick, trying my best to do it just as my mother did. She would so carefully outline her lips, then carefully fill them in. When she was done, she would rub her lips together to make sure it was all perfectly blended. It was a well-choreographed routine. She never left the house to go anywhere without putting on her "face," and doing her hair. I followed her example, of course. I never leave the house, even to go to the gym, unless my lipstick is in place. I keep a mirror compact and lipstick in my purse for re-application as needed.

—Jamie H., Birmingham, Alabama

I remember always having a gloss in my pocket. I could not wear lipstick growing up, but gloss was always okay with Mom. To this day, I love to always have a shine on my lips and a gloss stick in my pocket. I have a gloss in so many colors—red, pink, peach, orange—and then of course lip balm. I think I will add a shine now!

—Sandy T., Pottsboro, Texas

Acknowledgments

There are so many people I'm grateful to have in my life, it's impossible to know where to begin!

To all of the people I've met in my travels who have changed the trajectory of my life in the most delightfully unexpected ways;

To my readers who packed their mental suitcases and meandered with me on this transformative and revitalizing journey;

To my exceptionally clever and talented editor Laura Matthews at www.thinkStory.biz for her sage advice and keen insight;

To my meticulous and enthusiastic illustrator Lesley Vernon at www.lvdesignhouse.com for her magical ability to draw glimpses into my soul;

To my conscientious and brilliant book designer and producer Carol Hohle at www.CarolHohle.com for her superior skill and masterful expertise;

To the lovely ladies who shared their lipstick memories for this book and the many more ladies who will be posting on my "Lipstick Ladies League" Facebook group page;

To my mamma, who has always made me feel beautiful and extraordinary;

To my daughter, who makes me feel loved and appreciated;

And to my dear and precious husband, who's been traveling with me for thirty-four years and giving me all the hugs I need when I need them;

Without all of you, there would be no reason to wear lipstick and no reason to write about lipstick. Y'all have been my inspiration and motivation. I love you to the moon and back again and again!

About the Author

Author, publisher and women's retreat host, Annette Bridges is on a mission to help every woman realize her story is extraordinary, valuable and noteworthy. She publishes books, journals and coloring books that empower, encourage and entertain. Annette's retreats provide women an oasis to decompress, rediscover their inner child and learn what their hearts desire most.

Before writing books, this former public school and homeschool educator spent a decade writing hundreds of helpful, instructive, and light-hearted columns published by Texas newspapers, parenting magazines, websites and bloggers.

Writing aspirations began as a child with journal keeping, but Annette would not write her first published essay – a guest column in the Dallas Morning News – until she became an empty nester when her only child left for college. Annette went from a brand new empty nest mom wondering what in the heck she was going to do next in her life to a prolific writer.

Annette lives on a cattle ranch with her husband John, dachshund Lady and lots of cows. She can drive a tractor but only if wearing a fresh coat of lipstick and it's not her pedicure day!

You can learn more about Annette's books, blogs and videos as well as her women's retreats at www.annettebridges.com. She invites you to follow her and chat on Facebook at www.facebook.com/TexasAuthorAnnetteBridges

About the Illustrator

Lesley Vernon is an artist, illustrator, and graphic designer from the Philadelphia area. From a young age, Lesley has loved drawing and doodling, filling the pages of many sketchbooks. She credits an enthusiastic high school art teacher for inspiring her to pursue art more seriously. After earning a bachelor's degree in studio art, Lesley has worked in a variety of artistic avenues, including print, web, illustration, and vinyl decals. She loves sharing art with her two young sons Mason and Ryder by coloring, painting, and other hands-on crafts. You can reach Lesley by email at lesley@lvdesignhouse.com, or see more of her work on her website at www.lvdesignhouse.com.

www.ingramcontent.com/pod-product-compliance
Lightning Source LLC
Chambersburg PA
CBHW070628300426
44113CB00010B/1694